P9-CKN-844

THE
ANCIENT
HEBREWS

CULTURES
OF THE PAST

THE ANCIENT HEBREWS

KENNY MANN

BENCHMARK BOOKS

MARSHALL CAVENDISH
NEW YORK

Benchmark Books
Marshall Cavendish Corporation
99 White Plains Road
Tarrytown, New York 10591-9001

Library of Congress Cataloging-in-Publication Data
Mann, Kenny.
   The ancient Hebrews / Kenny Mann.
      p.   cm. — (Cultures of the past)
   Includes bibliographical references and index.
   Summary: Examines the history, culture, religion, daily life, and legends of the
Jewish people.
   ISBN 0-7614-0302-7 (lb)
   1. Jews—History—To 70 A.D.—Juvenile literature. 2. Bible. O.T.—History
of Biblical events—Juvenile literature. [1. Jews—History. 2. Bible. O.T.—
History of Biblical events.] I. Title. II. Series.
DS118.M256   1999
909'.04924—DC21   97-6551

Printed in Hong Kong

Book design by Carol Matsuyama
Photo research by Debbie Needleman

Front cover: Miriam and other Hebrew women dance with joy after crossing the
     Red Sea. Detail from *The Song of Joy,* by James Tissot (1836–1902).
Back cover: A modern scholar in Jerusalem.

CONTENTS

CHAPTER ONE

IN THE BEGINNING

"Get thee out of thy country and from thy kindred, and from thy father's house, unto the land that I will show thee."* According to Jewish tradition, this is the message that Abraham, the first Hebrew in recorded history, received from God. Together with his father, Terah; his wife, Sarah; and his nephew Lot, he had left his native city of Ur in ancient Babylonia and traveled north to the city of Haran in Mesopotamia. By the very act of crossing the Euphrates River, the family group became identified in the Bible as *Ivrim,* or Hebrews, "the people who crossed over."

Abraham was 75 years old when God ordered him to leave Haran and travel to a destination that God would make known to him. On this journey God made a Covenant, or sacred pact, with Abraham. He promised that if Abraham would obey God's laws, he and his descendants would become God's Chosen People and God would give them a land that would be theirs forever. The Bible tells us that Abraham lived to be 175 and to lead his people from Mesopotamia into Canaan, the Promised Land.

Did Abraham and his family really exist? Did these events really happen? We may never know. While these questions may occupy scholars of world history, for Jews they are a matter of faith. Ever since ancient times, the Jews' belief in their Covenant with God and their bond with the Promised Land—received through Abraham—has formed the central core of their religion and culture. It is still the pivot around which Jewish history spins.

*All biblical quotations are from the *Holy Bible,* New International Version.

The Promised Land

Although the history of the early Hebrews centered on the land of Canaan, it played itself out in the broader context of the Fertile Crescent. This is a band of cultivable land that starts at the head of the Persian Gulf, where the Tigris and Euphrates Rivers empty their waters. It follows the two rivers northward through ancient Babylonia (in present-day southeastern

Abraham and his people make their way to the Promised Land. In this nineteenth-century engraving, the travelers resemble nomads of the Arabian Desert. Modern research, however, has shown that camels were not used in this region until around the third century C.E.—some two thousand years after Abraham made his epic journey.

Iraq) and Mesopotamia (in northwestern Iraq) to the plains of Anatolia (southeastern Turkey). From there it bends to the southwest, following the Mediterranean seaboard through ancient Canaan (present-day Syria, Lebanon, Israel, and Jordan) and finally losing itself in the wastes of the Sinai Peninsula. In ancient times Canaan formed a land bridge between Mesopotamia and Egypt, linking the continents of Africa and Asia.

There cannot be many places on earth where one could "kill a lion on a day when snow fell," yet such an incident is described in the Bible. It indicates the extraordinarily diverse landscape that Abraham and his family found when they entered Canaan sometime between the nineteenth and sixteenth centuries B.C.E.*

The Promised Land, located in southern Canaan, was only about 400 miles (644 kilometers) long and 100 miles (161 kilometers) wide. To the

*Many systems of dating have been used by different cultures throughout history. This series of books uses B.C.E. (Before Common Era) and C.E. (Common Era) instead of B.C. (Before Christ) and A.D. (Anno Domini) out of respect for the diversity of the world's peoples.

THE BIBLE AS HISTORY

To many Jews and Christians the Old Testament represents a historical and spiritual truth that is not to be questioned. To many other readers it is an extraordinary work of literature. To historians, however, the material presents a fascinating collection of facts, conflicting information, and disconnected stories. So far archaeologists and other specialists have found little evidence for biblical events before about 1000 B.C.E. In fact, these ancient tales have raised more questions than answers.

What exactly were the origins of the ancient Hebrews, for example? Were they Amorites from distant Babylonia? Or had they always lived in Canaan, set apart from other inhabitants because of their unique belief system?

Who was Moses? He was raised as an Egyptian yet came to the rescue of a Hebrew slave. He could not have spoken Hebrew yet was chosen to lead the Israelites out of Egypt. The Bible suggests that a million or more people followed Moses. Yet there are no Egyptian records of such a mass migration, nor could the desert have supported so many.

Were those who followed Abraham and those who followed Moses four hundred years later perhaps two very different groups of people whom Moses united under his leadership? And could the amazing life spans of the patriarchs and matriarchs actually symbolize several periods in history?

Perhaps the ancient soils of the Near East will one day reveal their secrets.

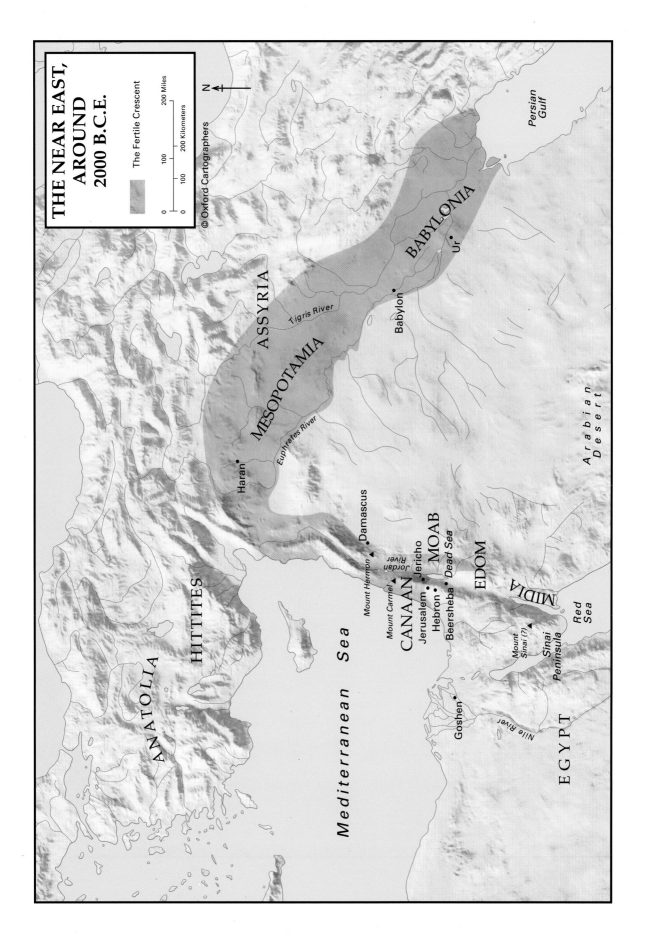

THE NEAR EAST,
AROUND
2000 B.C.E.

The Fertile Crescent

200 Miles
200 Kilometers
100
100
0
0

N

© Oxford Cartographers

Persian
Gulf

BABYLONIA

Ur

ASSYRIA

Tigris River

Babylon

MESOPOTAMIA

Euphrates River

Haran

Arabian
Desert

Damascus

Mount Hermon

Jordan River

MOAB

Jericho

Mount Carmel

Dead Sea

Jerusalem

EDOM

CANAAN

Hebron

Beersheba

MIDIA

ANATOLIA

HITTITES

Mount Sinai (?)

Sinai
Peninsula

Red
Sea

Mediterranean
Sea

Goshen

Nile River

EGYPT

The Promised Land enjoyed a good climate, and its fertile soil gave rise to abundant crops.

west lay the Mediterranean Sea; to the east, the hostile sands of the Arabian Desert. The narrow coastal belt enjoyed an almost tropical climate, in which palm trees flourished. Farther east lay fertile hills rich in various crops. From these cultivated slopes the land rose to the Judean Hills, some 3,000 feet (914 meters) above sea level, where winter snowfall was not uncommon. These descended to the barren "wilderness" of the Bible — a rocky desert inhabited only by nomads with their flocks of sheep and goats. A few miles farther east lay the hot and steamy valley of the Jordan River. Beyond that, the land rose again 3,000 feet (914 meters) to the Transjordanian highlands. In a north-south direction, the terrain was equally broken. Less than 150 miles (241 kilometers) separated Mount Hermon in the north, rising 9,000 feet (2,743 meters) above sea level, from the Dead Sea to the south, lying 1,300 feet (396 meters) below sea level.

The people whom Abraham encountered in Canaan were as diverse as the landscape. Some lived in small cities; others were farmers or nomads. Some were native to the area; others had migrated from neighboring regions. Almost all spoke Aramaic or one of the many related Semitic* dialects.

The Canaanites knew how to reap the benefits of their fertile hills and

*About two hundred years ago a historian invented the term "Semitic" for those peoples believed to be the descendants of Shem, the son of Noah. Among them are the Hebrews, Amorites, Arabs, and many other peoples who spoke or speak Aramaic and related languages.

valleys. Sinuhe, an Egyptian traveler in the nineteenth century B.C.E., wrote, "It was a good land. . . . Figs were in it, and grapes. Plentiful was its honey, abundant its olives. Every kind of fruit was on its trees. Barley was there, and summer wheat. There was no limit to any kind of cattle." In the hill regions cedar forests flourished. This timber was sought after by the rulers of Mesopotamia and Egypt, where wood for building was scarce.

Sandwiched between the continents, Canaan inevitably became a major thoroughfare for traders. Small ports along the Mediterranean harbored ships from Egypt, Europe, and Anatolia. Ships also plied the Red Sea to the Indian Ocean and the Persian Gulf, forming trade links with Africa, Asia, and the Far East. Inland three major international trade routes passed through Canaan, connecting the coast with the interior and with the lands to the north and south.

The Canaanites made large profits from trade, but these came at a heavy price. Its location made Canaan not only a thriving center of commerce but also a prize coveted by the imperial powers of the time. They turned the "land of milk and honey" into a vast battleground. The history of the Canaanites thus was written not so much by themselves as by those who conquered Canaan, among them the Egyptians, Assyrians, Philistines, Babylonians, Persians, Greeks, and Romans. It was against this complex background that the ancient Hebrews carved out their destiny.

Abraham, Isaac, and Jacob: The Patriarchs

According to the Bible, Abraham was the founder and first patriarch of the Jewish nation. He was a ninth-generation descendant of Shem, the son of Noah, builder of the ark. Abraham is described as a "sojourner" or tent dweller. Most likely he and his family rode donkeys (camels were not used in the area until much later), traveling with their flocks of sheep and goats much as seminomadic people still do in parts of the Middle East. Abraham obeyed God's command to leave his native land and travel "unto the land that I will show thee." He traveled widely through Canaan, into Egypt, and back into Canaan, setting up altars at various places. There was much conflict between Abraham and the Canaanites, but eventually he "became rich in livestock, silver, and gold" (Genesis 13:2) and made a permanent camp near Hebron.

According to the Bible, God promised to give Abraham and Sarah a son, but Sarah was 90 and her husband was 99 before that son, Isaac, was born! Sarah, the first matriarch of Jewish history, died at the age of 127. Before he died at age 175, Abraham remarried and had several more children.

Like Abraham, Isaac, the second patriarch, was entrusted by God to keep the holy Covenant. He married Rebecca, known as the second matriarch, and she gave birth to twins, Esau and Jacob. These two sons became bitter rivals for their father's wealth and for the task of fulfilling the Covenant. Torn with jealousy, Esau vowed to kill his brother, and Jacob fled far north, to Paddan-Aram, where the family had kin.

Jacob spent twenty years at Paddan-Aram. He married Rachel and her sister, Leah (Hebrew men had many wives and concubines), and fathered twelve sons and a daughter, Dinah. Jacob once dreamed that he struggled with an angel of God. When Jacob finally returned to Canaan with his large family, God renamed him Israel, or "he who has wrestled with God." Jacob was the third Hebrew patriarch and, according to the Bible, he lived to be 147. His sons became the founders of the twelve Hebrew tribes, or the Israelites, known in the Bible as the B'nai Yisrael, or the "children of Israel." Jews today are more commonly called 'Am Yisrael—"the people of Israel."*

Joseph: Interpreter of Dreams

Joseph was Jacob's favorite son, and his brothers were jealous of him. After Joseph told his brothers that he had dreamed they would one day bow down to him, they kidnapped him and sold him into slavery in Egypt. At this time—around 1650 B.C.E.—Egypt was ruled by Asiatic people known as the Hyksos (Hick-sohs). Through his ability to correctly interpret dreams, Joseph came to the Hyksos pharaoh's notice and rose to a powerful position in government.

Several years later Canaan was struck by famine, and Joseph's father, Jacob, was forced to migrate to Egypt with

*Abraham and his descendants are known as the Hebrews. Once Jacob, also called Israel, founded the twelve tribes or "children of Israel," his people also became known as the Israelites. In the Bible's Book of Esther, which describes events of the fifth century B.C.E., the Israelites are called the Yehudim, or "Jews." This originally referred to the inhabitants of Judah, or "Judeans," but has come to refer to Jews in general.

his family. Joseph recognized the brothers who had sold him into bondage and forgave them. The Hyksos pharaoh allowed them to settle in a place called Goshen. According to the Bible, the Israelites remained there for four hundred years, multiplying and prospering, as God had promised they would.

Moses and Joshua: Into the Promised Land

Around 1315 B.C.E. a new dynasty of powerful pharaohs rose in Egypt, among them Ramses I, Seti I, and Ramses II. These kings conquered the Hyksos and enslaved them, along with many other peoples, including the Hebrews, who had been under Hyksos rule. The slaves were forced to build huge monuments and new cities. Their lives were ones of unceasing toil and starvation.

One of the pharaohs—perhaps Ramses II (reigned 1279–1212 B.C.E.)—feared that the Israelites would one day turn against him. The pharaoh decreed that all male Hebrew infants were to be drowned at birth. According to the Bible, the pharaoh's

In this painting, Hebrew slaves move a sphinx to a temple in ancient Egypt. The nineteenth-century artist captured the slaves' exhaustion and the brutality of the overseers with their whips.

daughter found one such child in a basket, afloat on the Nile. She adopted him, named him Moses, and raised him as an Egyptian prince.

Moses always fought against injustice. One day he killed an Egyptian overseer who was beating a Hebrew slave. Moses had to flee for his life. He became a shepherd in Midian, in southeastern Sinai. While tending his flocks there, Moses first heard the voice of God, who ordered him to return to Egypt to demand the freedom of the Israelites.

"Let my people go!" Moses risked his life when he confronted the pharaoh with this request. But the pharaoh refused, and the Bible tells us that God then unleashed a series of ten plagues on Egypt. First the Nile turned to blood, a profound symbol of the thousands of infants drowned in its waters. Then massive infestations of frogs, lice, and swarming insects were followed by deadly disease, boils, hailstorms, locusts, and three days of absolute darkness. Only when the last plague killed all the firstborn sons of the Egyptians did the pharaoh allow the Israelites to leave.

This moment in Jewish history is known as the Exodus, or departure. The Israelites now numbered many thousands of people, and for the next forty years they followed Moses through the desert. He led them to the edge of Canaan, where he died in about 1220 B.C.E. The Bible gives his age as 120.

When the Israelites entered the Promised Land at last, it was under the leadership of the young warrior Joshua. Moses and Joshua had assigned ten of the twelve tribes to the northern part of Canaan, called Israel; two tribes would take the south, called Judah. The Israelites were no match for the well-trained Canaanite soldiers, who had iron armor and fast chariots. Instead of challenging the Canaanites in open battle, the Israelites lured them into the hills, where their chariots were useless. They plundered the Canaanites' cattle and crops, leaving them without food. The Israelites' spying and surprise attacks brought down major cities. They also exploited the lack of unity among Canaanite forces to divide enemy loyalties. Thus Joshua gradually entered and infiltrated the Promised Land.

Judges and Kings

During this period elders dispensed justice within each Israelite tribe. A higher authority, however, were the so-called *shoftim,* or "judges." These men and women were held accountable to God. In war they functioned as generals; in peace they were more like presidents.

The Israelites capture the Canaanite city of Jericho. Following God's command, the Hebrews marched around the city for six days. On the seventh day, Joshua's priests blew their trumpets, the Hebrews shouted, and the walls of Jericho collapsed.

Twelve judges ruled the Israelites during the twelfth and eleventh centuries B.C.E. They were mainly occupied with fighting the Philistines, a people from Crete or Cyprus who had invaded Canaan. The Bible depicts the judges as larger-than-life figures. One of the best-known judges was Samson, a long-haired folk hero of fabulous strength who was reputed to have killed a thousand Philistines with the jawbone of an ass.

Despite the system of judges, however, the Israelites had no central leadership. They needed a united military front to drive the Philistines out of their hills. Their first king, Saul, was selected by the prophet Samuel around 1000 B.C.E. Two years later, when Saul fell in battle, the Israelites chose David as their leader. He belonged to the tribe of Judah, the largest of the twelve Israelite tribes. David is known as the greatest of the forty-two kings and queens who ruled the Israelites.

David and Solomon: Unity and Division

In a popular story about David as a young boy, he topples the giant Philistine warrior Goliath with a single stone shot from a sling. When he became king in 1004 B.C.E., David defeated the Philistines and took over all the regions still in the hands of the Canaanites. He captured the city of Jerusalem, where he built his

Goliath was over nine feet tall and wore a bronze helmet and coat of armor. David faced him armed only with his shepherd's staff, his sling, and his faith in God. One well-aimed shot at the giant's forehead brought Goliath down. Then David pulled the giant's sword from its scabbard and cut off his enemy's head.

palace and housed the Ark of the Covenant, the holy symbol of the Hebrews. Thus he made the city both the political and religious capital of the Israelites. By the time David died in 965 B.C.E., his kingdom, which united Israel and Judah, extended from Mesopotamia to the Red Sea.

David's son Solomon, who became the next king, nurtured the kingdom through extensive peace and trade treaties. He controlled all the trade routes connecting Mesopotamia, Syria, Arabia, and Egypt. From Sheba in southern Arabia came frankincense, spices, and myrrh. Solomon traded oil and grains with the Phoenicians, whose land bordered Israel, in return for cedarwood and other raw materials for his building projects. From the East African coast he imported gold, ivory, and rare animals for the royal zoo. From Asia Minor came copper, iron, and horses. From Egypt came ceremonial chariots.

It is said that around 1000 B.C.E., Queen Makeda of the Ethiopian province of Sheba visited King Solomon in Israel to learn some of his legendary wisdom and, probably, to arrange lucrative trade agreements. They fell in love, and when Makeda returned to Ethiopia, she gave birth to their son, Menelik. For seven hundred years, Ethiopian rulers were considered the direct descendants of this union. In this sixteenth-century painting, Makeda presents gifts to the king.

The Israelites were no longer a nomadic people. Numbering some 800,000 at this time, they had become farmers and city dwellers. For the first time Israel was a power to be reckoned with in the Middle East. But this prosperity was to be short-lived.

Solomon's trade and development policies required an army, to ensure peace, as well as thousands of bureaucrats, to impose taxes and tolls on trade goods. In addition, 30,000 men were practically enslaved for several years to build a magnificent temple in Jerusalem for the Ark of the Covenant. Solomon drove the kingdom to the verge of bankruptcy, and the seeds were ripe for rebellion. When he died in 928 B.C.E., the Israelites had little patience for his cruel and arrogant son, Rehoboam. The ten tribes that occupied the northern region, known as Israel, refused Rehoboam's leadership and broke away from the kingdom. The two remaining tribes continued to occupy Judah, their homeland to the south. From then on, Israel and Judah remained separate, each with its own king.

In 722 B.C.E. Israel was overrun by Assyria. The people of the ten tribes were deported from their own land and never heard of again. The tiny state of Judah lasted until 586 B.C.E., when it was conquered by Nebuchadrezzar, king of Babylonia. He destroyed the city of Jerusalem and the great temple that Solomon had built. He also exiled most of the state's citizens to Babylonia, leaving only the poorest Israelites behind. But the people of Judah did not disappear. They thrived in Babylonia, where they kept their faith and culture alive.

Return from Exile

In 539 B.C.E. Cyrus, the king of Persia, conquered Babylonia. It was to his advantage to rebuild the ravaged state of Judah, now under his rule. Cyrus encouraged the exiled Israelites to return, providing them with funds and supplies. About 40,000 Israelites took up his offer. Back in Jerusalem they set about painstakingly rebuilding their devastated land and building the Second Temple, which was completed in 515 B.C.E.

Despite several setbacks Jerusalem once again flowered as the Israelites' holy city, and Judah eventually prospered. In 332 B.C.E. the Persian Empire fell to the armies of the Greek conqueror Alexander the Great. His troops swept through Egypt, Judah, and Syria and as far east as India, gathering lands and peoples into the mighty Greek empire. The conquerors

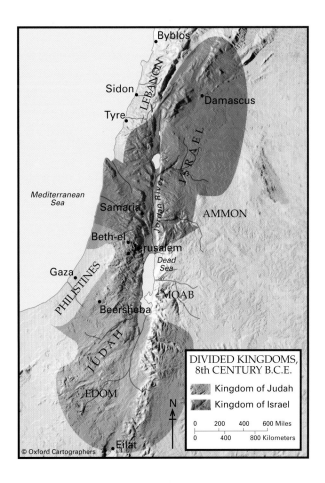

DIVIDED KINGDOMS,
8th CENTURY B.C.E.

Kingdom of Judah

Kingdom of Israel

brought with them their Greek language, ideas, and beliefs. In time their culture, known as Hellenism, was adopted throughout the empire.

While some Jews, as they were now called, welcomed Hellenism, others were violently opposed to the new ideas. In 175 B.C.E. the tyrannical Syrian king Antiochus Epiphanes (ant-EYE-uh-kus ih-PIH-fuh-neez) attempted to establish Hellenism in Judah by condemning practicing Jews to death. This sparked a revolution led by a farmer-priest named Mattathias and his five sons. They were driven by dreams not of wealth or power but of religious freedom. In a guerrilla war that lasted more than ten years, Mattathias's followers won battle after battle, hammering relentlessly at the Syrians' vastly superior forces. For this reason they became known as the

THE HELLENISTIC WAY OF LIFE

The Hellenistic Age (333–30 B.C.E.) brought together the ideas and cultures of Greece, Persia, Egypt, and India in a great flowering of art and thought. Throughout Alexander the Great's empire Jews were exposed to the Greek way of life. In time Jewish businessmen adopted the practices, manners, and even the clothing of their Greek partners. Jewish youths met at the gymnasium to practice sports and discuss philosophy with their Greek friends. Jewish women copied the robes and hairstyles of fashionable Greek ladies. Many Jews began to speak Greek rather than Aramaic or Hebrew, and some even took Greek names. The Greeks also brought with them improved methods of agriculture, sophisticated town planning, and their distinctive art and architecture.

The groundbreaking philosophies of Plato, Socrates, and Aristotle; the great mathematical advances of Euclid and Pythagoras; the genius of Hippocrates in medicine; the tragedies and comedies of Euripides and Aristophanes—the Jews absorbed these and other influences, applying Greek logic and reason to find ever deeper meaning in their faith.

Maccabe'im (mah-kah-BEH-im), from the Hebrew word for "hammerers." In 164 B.C.E. the Maccabees reclaimed Jerusalem. In 143 B.C.E. they signed peace treaties with the Syrians. The impossible had been achieved: for the second time the kingdom of Judah rose again.

Triumph of the Romans

Unfortunately, Jewish independence was once again short-lived. Mattathias's descendants quarreled bitterly over the throne of Judah, plunging the nation into civil war. In the meantime Rome had risen to conquer the Greek empire that Alexander had founded. In 63 B.C.E. the Roman general Gnaeus Pompeius (GNEYE-us pahm-PAY-us) stormed Jerusalem, marching into the holiest room of the Temple. Judah had fallen again. It now became known by its Latin name, Judea.

Only forty years later the Romans did away with Jewish kings altogether and sent their own governors, or procurators, to administer their vassal state. These corrupt officials saw Judea as a means of feathering their own nests. They imposed harsh taxes, stole the nation's wealth, and tried to eliminate Judaism altogether.

Again rebellion seethed among the Jews. They were already split into various groups with differing beliefs. Some favored adapting to Roman rule. Others, known as Zealots, vowed to reclaim religious and

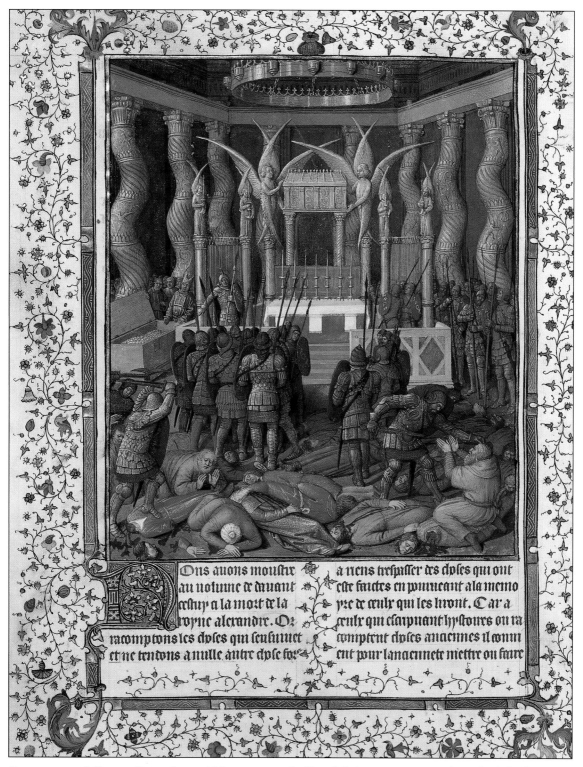

Ons auons moustre
au uolume de diuant
cessuy a la mort de la
royne alexandre. Or
racomptons les choses qui seusuiuet
et ne tendons a nulle autre chose for:

a riens trespasser des choses qui ont
este faictes en pruncant ala memo
yre de ceulx qui les liront. Car a
ceulx qui escripuant hystoires ou ra
comptent choses anciennes il conui
ent pour lanciennete mettre ou faire

Roman general Gnaeus Pompeius and his men enter the Temple's inner sanctuary, where the Ark of the Covenant was kept. The Jews were so shocked that no one stopped him—an embarrassment to Jews to this day.

political freedom. Using cloak-and-dagger tactics, the Zealots murdered Romans as well as those Jews who cooperated with the conquerors. In retaliation the Romans crucified between 50,000 and 100,000 Jews, including the Jewish teacher Jesus Christ.

In 66 C.E. Florus, the last Roman procurator, conducted pagan rites in the Temple and raided its treasury for funds for the Roman emperor. He offended the Jews' most sacred beliefs so deeply that rival factions joined forces with the Zealots and wiped out the Roman garrison at the Temple. The news spread like wildfire, and in every village and outpost

of Judea, Jews rose in arms against the vastly superior Roman armies. In northern Judea 80,000 crack Roman troops slaughtered or captured and sold into slavery 100,000 Jews. At Jerusalem the Roman general Titus tried to intimidate the Jews by displaying thousands of battering rams while 70,000 foot soldiers and 10,000 horsemen swept past the city. For two weeks catapults hurled huge rocks at Jerusalem, tearing gaping holes in the walls. But in hand-to-hand combat the Jews—who numbered only 20,000—drove the Romans back. Deciding to starve out the Jews, Titus built a vast earthen wall around the city.

Inside Jerusalem chaos reigned. In uncontrolled fury the Zealots killed Jews who supported peace with the Romans. The stench of the bodies of those who had died from starvation and plague filled the air. The end was inevitable. In 70 C.E., after four years of siege, the Romans set the Temple on fire and razed it to the ground.

To symbolize their triumph, the Romans changed the name of the conquered nation from Judea to Palestine*, after the Philistines. But although Jerusalem and its Temple had been destroyed, the Jewish people still had their faith. Those who survived carried it to the four corners of the earth, where it continues to outlive all attempts at defeat.

*The Promised Land had been known as Canaan until Joshua divided part of it into the provinces of Judah and Israel. Under David these provinces were united as the kingdom of Israel, which was divided again into separate kingdoms under Rehoboam. Israel was destroyed by the Assyrians, while Judah survived to become first Judea and then, under the Romans, Palestine.

During the siege of Jerusalem, many Zealots escaped to the stronghold of Masada, built on a towering plateau near the Dead Sea. When the Romans attacked Masada in 73 C.E., they found the fortress silent. More than one thousand Jewish men, women, and children had committed suicide rather than fall into Roman hands. The ruins of Masada still stand.

CHAPTER TWO

A LIVING FAITH

Jewish history and religion begin with Abraham and the Covenant he made with God. When Abraham left Ur around 1900 B.C.E., he undoubtedly carried with him a set of beliefs from Babylonia. Like many other pagan cultures all over the world, the Babylonians believed in gods and goddesses who behaved just like human beings, except that they were immortal and had more power. These gods were not universal; rather, they favored only the people who worshipped them. The stories, or myths, about these gods symbolized the awe-inspiring mystery of natural events, such as the beginning of all things and the cycle of life and death.

Pagans feared their gods. The pagan gods had power over life and death, health and sickness, wealth and poverty, war and peace, fertility, rain, harvests, and every other aspect of life on earth, in the heavens, and in the underworld. People naturally sought the best possible relationship with these gods. They believed that through worship, gifts of food, and especially through sacrifices—sometimes of human beings—they could communicate with the gods and win their favor. Gifts were offered to statues or images of the gods, which worshippers kept in their temples and homes.

Pagan beliefs ruled people's lives in ancient Mesopotamia and Canaan. Once he had received the Covenant, however, Abraham revealed an extraordinary new vision to his people: *there in fact was only one God, who chose the Hebrews as his people.* This God was invisible and all-powerful. He needed no images or idols. From now on, the Hebrews could carry God in their hearts.

In time the Hebrew belief system came to be known as monotheism, from Greek words meaning "a single god." Monotheism was Abraham's · legacy to humankind, for from his belief emerged not only Judaism but also Christianity and Islam, the two other great monotheistic religions of the world.

THE *ENUMA ELISH—* THE BABYLONIAN CREATION MYTH

Almost certainly Abraham would have been familiar with the *Enuma Elish*, the Babylonian creation myth:

When on high the heaven had not been named
Firm ground below had not been called by name
There was naught but Apsu, their begetter
And Mummu-Tiamat, she who bore them all . . .

From a formless waste emerge Apsu (fresh water), his wife Tiamat (the salty sea), and Mummu, the womb of chaos. Other gods are born from them and rise in battle against their parents in the struggle between order and chaos. In retaliation Tiamat brings forth a host of monsters to fight on her behalf, among them Great-Lion, Mad-Dog, and Scorpion-Man. At last Ea (the earth) fathers the sun god Marduk. "Four were his eyes, four were his ears. When he moved his lips, fire blazed forth."

Marduk rules over a host of lesser gods and establishes order in the world. In his honor the gods build the great ziggurat at Babylon—"the earthly temple, symbol of infinite heaven." From Babylon "the universe receives its structure, the hidden world is made plain and the gods are assigned their places in the universe."

Two Names, One God

Before making his Covenant with God, Abraham was a pagan, like the rest of his contemporaries. He may have believed in Baal, the Canaanite god of fertility, or in Marduk, the Babylonian sun god. But the god who was heard by Abraham was the Canaanite "high god" El, who revealed himself as El Shaddai, or "El of the Mountain." The Bible portrays El as a god who sometimes came to Abraham as a voice or an angel. Such appearances, known as epiphanies or revelations, were not uncommon in the pagan world.

Abraham was not the only person to know El, but he was the only person *chosen* by El for a Covenant. The Covenant promised that Abraham would found a great nation whose seed would be "more numerous than the stars." It guaranteed the Hebrews—the Chosen People—

God's special protection forever. In return the Covenant demanded only three things: that El would be recognized as the one god of the Hebrews, that all Hebrew males would be circumcised eight days after birth as a sign of the Covenant, and that the Hebrews would cease the pagan ritual of human sacrifice. In these ways El showed how he differed from pagan gods and how the Hebrews differed from other folk.

Abraham's son Isaac and his grandson Jacob also experienced various epiphanies. Jacob once slept near the Jordan River, using a stone as a pillow. He dreamed of a great ladder on which angels trod between heaven and earth. El stood at the top and repeated to Jacob the promises he had made to Abraham. Those promises had been made only to the Hebrews in Canaan. This time El promised Jacob his protection not only in Canaan but *wherever Jacob might go*. In other words, the Hebrew concept of God was beginning to broaden.

When Jacob awoke from his dream, he was filled with awe. He upended his sleeping stone, anointed it with oil, and renamed the holy place Beth'el, the "House of El." The ancient name of El survives today in many Hebrew names, including Israel and Ishmael.

In the Hebrew Bible El is also referred to as Elohim, meaning "God"; as JHVH, meaning "Lord"; and as JHVH Elohim, meaning "Lord God." No one knows how *JHVH* was pronounced, since early written Hebrew had no vowels and it was forbidden to speak God's name. Today some people write *Jehovah*, or *Yahweh*. Yahweh's name appears more than seven thousand times in the Bible, and it is Yahweh, not El, who dominated Hebrew history from Jacob's time onward. Religious Jews today still do not pronounce the name of God. Instead they use the word *Hashem*, "the name," for *God*.

A Prophet Is Chosen

Like Abraham, Moses did not set out to become one of God's special messengers. He had fled Egypt and was living as a shepherd in the land of Midian, somewhere near modern Eilat. While Moses was tending his flocks one day, the Bible says, "an angel of the Lord appeared to him" in

Opposite: *Jacob dreams of a ladder on which angels climb to God, who renews his promise to the Hebrews. This fifteenth-century painting depicts the Old Testament story from a Christian viewpoint, with God holding a cross.*

the light of a bush that burned but was not consumed. God, or Yahweh, called Moses by name, and he replied, "*Hineni!*" ("Here I am!") — the response of many Hebrew prophets when God called them.

Yahweh said to Moses, "Come no nearer. Take off your shoes, for the place on which you stand is holy ground. I am the God of your father, the God of Abraham, the God of Isaac and the God of Jacob" (Exodus 3:5).

Were Yahweh and El one and the same god, as some traditions maintain? Were they, perhaps, a combination of ideas about God that had evolved over the eight hundred years since Abraham's first encounter with El? Or were they quite different gods, forged into one by the authors of the Bible? These are questions that occupy historians and theologians, and they may never be answered. The fact remains, however, that Moses obeyed *his* god's commands and lived to give the Hebrews—and the rest of the world—one of the greatest documents in history.

By the Finger of God

About seven weeks after Moses and the Israelites escaped from Egypt, they arrived at Mount Sinai, in the Sinai Peninsula. The Bible says that Moses climbed the mountain several times to commune with Yahweh. The last time he remained there for forty days and forty nights. When he returned, he triumphantly bore two stone tablets engraved with the laws known as the Ten Commandments.

The Ten Commandments have ingrained themselves so deeply in Western minds that it is hard for us to imagine how revolutionary they were. The ancient Mesopotamians, Canaanites, and Egyptians worshipped the idols of many pagan gods representing the forces of nature. The idea of not making "graven images" was totally alien to their most sacred practices. The Sabbath—a day of rest—was also an unfamiliar idea. More commonly people, especially slaves, were worked to the bone every day of their lives.

Opposite: *Moses descends Mount Sinai with the stone tablets bearing the Ten Commandments. This painting is by the great seventeenth-century Dutch artist Rembrandt.*

THE TEN COMMANDMENTS

1   *I am the Lord God; thou shalt have no other gods before me.*

2   *Thou shalt not make unto thee any graven image, or any likeness of what is in the heavens above, or on the earth below, or in the waters under the earth.*

3   *Thou shalt not utter the Lord thy God's name in vain.*

4   *Remember the Sabbath day and keep it holy. Six days thou shalt labor and do all thy work, but the seventh day is a Sabbath of the Lord your God.*

5   *Honor thy father and thy mother, that thou may long endure on the land which the Lord your God is giving thee.*

6   *Thou shalt not murder.*

7   *Thou shalt not commit adultery.*

8   *Thou shalt not steal.*

9   *Thou shalt not bear false witness against thy neighbor.*

10   *Thou shalt not covet thy neighbor's house, thou shalt not covet thy neighbor's wife, or his male or female slave, or his ox or his ass, or anything that is your neighbor's.*

Abraham's One God, El, had been a tribal deity, favoring the Hebrews alone. He did not rule out the existence of other gods. Moses's One God, Yahweh, had become universal, *there for the benefit of all humankind*, and he did not tolerate other gods. This idea was a monumental leap forward in human thought. People's faith was no longer bound to the gods of nature; it could soar into a higher realm. Yahweh existed to enlist human beings as partners, not slaves, in an effort to make the world a better place.

Torah: The Power of the Word

Some streams of Jewish tradition say that Moses also received the first five books of the Old Testament on Mount Sinai. These books are known as the Torah ("teaching") or the Law. The Torah covers Jewish history from Genesis (the creation of the world) through Exodus (the escape from Egypt), Leviticus (laws concerning Temple rituals), and Numbers (a census of the Israelites), to Deuteronomy, in which Moses bids farewell to his people before they cross into the Promised Land.

The Torah also contains numerous commandments that cover many aspects of Jewish life. These were not listed as commandments in the original Torah but were extracted from its stories by later religious leaders known as rabbis (RAB-eyes) and by scholars.

To Jews striving to follow God's commandments, the Written Torah was often confusing or lacked necessary details. Thus some Jews believe that Moses was simultaneously given the spoken or Oral Torah on Mount Sinai. He handed down these unwritten laws to his successor, Joshua, who transmitted them in turn to his successor and so on in an unbroken chain that continues to this day.

The Ark of the Covenant contained the stone tablets and other holy relics of the Hebrews. They carried it with them wherever they went, even into battle. Eventually it was placed in the sanctuary of the First Temple.

Many Paths

In ancient times Jews did not all share exactly the same ideas. During the Second Temple period (539 B.C.E.–70 C.E.), they broke up into various sects and cults. The Essenes, for example, wanted nothing to do with the Temple, which they felt had been corrupted. They lived in desert communes near the Dead Sea and hoped to find salvation through obedience to God. The Dead Sea Sect, probably an offshoot of the Essenes, also lived in caves in the desert. They left behind the famous Dead Sea

The Dead Sea Scrolls were found in several caves such as this one at Khirbat Qumran. They were written by the Essenes or a related cult and include the oldest known copies of all the books of the Old Testament except the Book of Esther.

This Dead Sea Scroll, written sometime between 150 B.C.E. and 68 C.E., is part of the Book of Isaiah.

Scrolls, which were discovered by a Bedouin shepherd in 1947.

For almost eighty years, from 140 to 63 B.C.E., kings descended from Mattathias, the Maccabee leader, ruled Judea. Because these kings came from a family of priests, they controlled the Temple as well as the government. Their followers formed a political party called the Sadducees. But most ordinary people, as well as scribes and teachers, joined a party called the Pharisees. The Pharisees kept themselves separate from government because they believed that, if one lived according to the Torah and heeded the word of God, there was no need for government.

The Sadducees believed that the Written Torah was the only Torah they needed to obey, and they did so to the letter. Unfortunately the Torah contained many laws that could lead to disaster when followed literally. For example, in Exodus 21:24 the Torah demands "an eye for an eye." Does this mean that a person blinded by another would have to blind his opponent in return? The Sadducees would say yes. The Pharisees would say that this law needed to be interpreted, that it meant that one should pay the monetary value of an eye. Hence, they believed in the Oral as well as the Written Torah.

The Pharisees also had some beliefs that were not mentioned in the Torah. For example, they believed that God would reward the just and punish the wicked in a life after death. Most importantly, they believed in the coming of a Messiah. This was to be a military leader who would free the Jews from Roman rule, bring exiled Jews back to the Promised Land, and introduce a new age of universal peace. He would be a descendant of David, the greatest king of the Jews.

The Sadducees maintained the Temple in Jerusalem and carried out all its rituals and sacrifices. When the Second Temple was destroyed in 70 C.E., their faith lost its center and purpose, and it died out shortly afterward. The center of Jewish life for the Pharisees, however, was not the Temple but the synagogue. The synagogue was a *bet tefillah*, or "house of prayer"; a *bet k'nesset*, or "house of assembly"; a *bet midrash*, or "house of study"; and a community center. Many synagogues were distributed throughout Israel. After the decline of the Sadducees the practices of the Pharisees became widely accepted. They are the intellectual and spiritual ancestors of all Jews today.

When the Jews returned to Israel from exile in Babylonia, they built the Second Temple on the same site as the First Temple, which had been destroyed by the Babylonians. The new temple was completed in 515 B.C.E. This model shows how it is thought to have looked before its later destruction by the Romans.

CHAPTER THREE

The Tellers and the Tales

The idols that pagans worshipped were images that people could see and touch. Their belief in these paintings and carvings and the gods they represented was expressed in special rites and rituals, in dance, music, sculpture, and painting. Often idols were housed in elaborate temples, which frequently became the spiritual centers of great cities. Thus pagan religious architecture and art were encouraged and flourished.

After God revealed himself to Abraham, however, the patriarch rejected idol worship. For the Hebrews, then, arts inspired by religion were discouraged. At the same time Abraham and his people were for many centuries a seminomadic folk, with no permanent homes. Instead of temples, wherever they were, they set up simple altars intended for worship without any images of God.

The Hebrews lived and breathed their God and in time, as we have seen, they began writing about him. Thus, while other ancient cultures left behind marvelous buildings and sophisticated art, pottery, and metal goods, few such traces of the early Hebrews have been found. Instead, theirs was a literary culture, based on the spoken and written word.

Tanakh: The Hebrew Bible

The Hebrew Bible, called the Old Testament by Christians, is known to Jews as the Tanakh (tah-NACH). It is both a historical document and one of the greatest works of literature the world has known. The Tanakh consists of three different sections. The first is the Torah, or Five Books of Moses. The second is the Nevi'im, or "Prophets," and the third is the Ketuvim, or "Writings."

Throughout ancient and modern Western civilization, the Tanakh has affected people's values and the way they think. Many people commonly use ideas and phrases from the Tanakh without realizing their origin. Proverbs 16:18 warns us that "Pride goes before a fall." Deuteronomy 8:3 tells us that "Man does not live by bread alone," while Ecclesiastes 1:9

teaches that "There is nothing new under the sun." Most basic of all to Western ethics is Cain's question about his brother, Abel: "Am I my brother's keeper?" (Genesis 4:9).

Words of Warning

The second section of books in the Tanakh is the Nevi'im, or "Prophets." In English *prophet* usually means "one who foresees the future," but the Hebrew word *navi* means "one who is called by God." Thus the true prophets—for there were many false ones—felt compelled to follow God's call and convey his message to the people. The prophets often answered God's call against their

From the ninth to sixth centuries B.C.E., prophets including Amos, Elijah, Jeremiah, and others felt called upon by God to deliver his word to the Hebrews. Their words form some of the most moving and dramatic passages in the Old Testament. This portrait of Amos is by Juan de Borgona (c. 1470–1535).

35

Eliezer Ben-Yehuda (1858–1922) was the father of modern Hebrew.

While its origins are obscure, Hebrew probably was widely spoken during biblical times. By 200 C.E., however, most Jews spoke Aramaic or Greek. For the next 1,600 years Hebrew lingered as the sacred language of the Torah, spoken and written only by rabbis and scholars. In later years eastern European Jews developed Yiddish, a hotchpotch of German, other European languages, and Hebrew. Jews in Spain spoke Ladino, a Spanish-Hebrew derivation. But in the 1880s Eliezer Ben-Yehuda, a Lithuanian Jew, made it his life's mission to revive Hebrew as the common language of the Jews in Palestine. He had to invent new words for modern objects such as the toothbrush and ideas such as democracy, and he spent years searching ancient texts in other Semitic languages for suitable word roots. Ben-Yehuda's single-minded efforts paid off. In 1922 modern Hebrew was declared one of Palestine's official languages, along with English and Arabic. Today Hebrew is spoken all over Israel, just as it was four thousand years ago.

Yiddish Words in English

bagel—a hard, glazed, doughnut-shaped roll
schlep—a long distance; to drag or haul

mensch—a good or decent person
maven—an expert

will and at the risk of their own lives. There were three major and twelve minor prophets, including one woman, Deborah. The words of the prophets were first preserved orally and later in writing. These writings clearly outline the progression in Hebrew thought from protest against local paganism and corruption to the teaching of a universal morality to all people.

In 871 B.C.E. Ahab became king of Israel. His wife Jezebel worshipped the fertility deities Baal and Asherah. Long-haired, clad only in a leather loincloth, the prophet Elijah tramped the countryside, denouncing the spreading paganism. He challenged the 450 priests of Baal to a competition on Mount Carmel. They were to slaughter a bull and call upon their gods to ignite the sacrificial fire beneath the meat. Elijah would do the same. Needless to say, the pagans' efforts were in vain. But when Elijah prayed, "the fire of the Lord fell and burned up the sacrifice, the wood, the stones, and the soil" (I Kings 18:38).

Later, in his moment of greatest despair, Elijah was called by the Lord

Jezebel, the vain and beautiful wife of King Ahab, provoked God's anger by persuading her husband to worship pagan idols. The queen later suffered a violent death, as foretold by the prophet Elijah.

to witness his passing on the mountain—not in a great wind, a mighty earthquake, or a raging fire, but in the soothing caress of a gentle breeze.

Later prophets, including the eighth-century B.C.E. shepherd Amos, protested against corruption and vice in the ruling class. "You trample on the poor and force him to give you grain. . . . You oppress the righteous and take bribes" (Amos 5:11-12). By this time the Israelites had come to believe not only that they possessed a great truth, but that they were responsible for sharing it with others. Thus Amos taught that the Lord had no need of the rituals of cult worship but demanded a higher standard of moral conduct.

The prophet Isaiah lived to see the Assyrians conquer the kingdom of Israel in 722 B.C.E. During this terrible time of war, Isaiah raged against his "sinful nation" and the "brood of evildoers" who would bring it down. But he also preached peace, and his most famous words are now engraved near the United Nations building in Manhattan: "Nation shall not lift up sword against nation, neither shall they learn war anymore" (Isaiah 2:4).

In exile in Babylonia, the prophet Ezekiel (ih-ZEE-kyuhl) had a vision in which God set him down in a valley of dry bones. When God breathed life into the bones, they reassembled as people, and God said, "These bones are the House of Israel" (Ezekiel 37:11). Ezekiel interpreted this to mean that eventually the Jewish state would be reborn.

Perhaps the clearest voice during the exile was that of a man whose name we do not know. The Unknown Prophet, as he is called, taught that the Jews were chosen by God to suffer their torments for the sake of all humankind. Through this suffering, the prophet said, the Jews would redeem all people in the eyes of God— an idea that has haunted the Jews throughout their history.

Of Songs and Stories

The Ketuvim, or "Writings"—the third section of the Tanakh—contains a variety of works that tell the story of the Hebrews up to the time of the Greek empire in the fourth century B.C.E.

Most of the 150 psalms, or religious poems, of the Ketuvim are attributed to King David, of the tenth century B.C.E. David was a renowned musician and may have accompanied his psalms with music. The most famous is perhaps Psalm 23, which begins, "The Lord is my shepherd, I

shall not want." A later psalm, written by another author during the Babylonian exile, mourns the lost land of Zion (Israel).

Included in the Ketuvim are three works attributed by biblical scholars to Solomon. In his youth, it is said, Solomon wrote

In Ezekiel's vision the dead came back to life—just as, the prophet believed, the Jews would return to the land of Israel after years of exile in Babylonia.

39

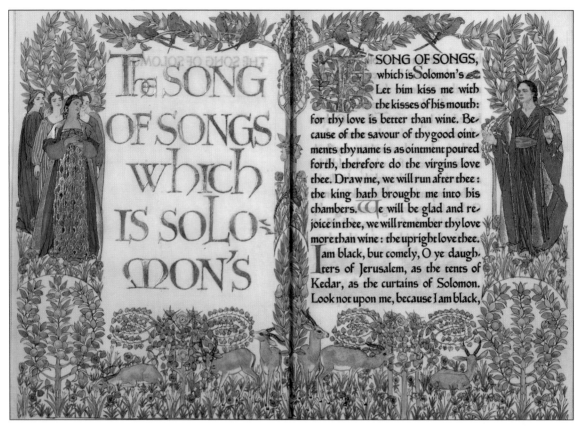

SONG OF SONGS,
which is Solomon's
Let him kiss me with
the kisses of his mouth:
for thy love is better than wine. Because of the savour of thy good ointments thy name is as ointment poured forth, therefore do the virgins love thee. Draw me, we will run after thee: the king hath brought me into his chambers. We will be glad and rejoice in thee, we will remember thy love more than wine: the upright love thee. I am black, but comely, O ye daughters of Jerusalem, as the tents of Kedar, as the curtains of Solomon. Look not upon me, because I am black,

The Old Testament's Song of Solomon is a collection of love poems that some scholars believe represent God's love for Israel.

the Song of Songs, an exquisite love poem. The Proverbs, a collection of sayings explaining the meaning of life and of human relations, are attributed to Solomon's middle years. In his old age Solomon lamented the futility of everything in life in the gloomy book of Ecclesiastes: "All things are wearisome, more than one can say" (Ecclesiastes 1:8).

The well-known story of Ruth is a lovely tale of the deep friendship between Ruth, a gentile widow, and her Jewish mother-in-law, Naomi. In the story Ruth eventually converts to Judaism, saying to Naomi, "Your people shall be my people, and your God my God" (Ruth 1:16). David, who became king of Israel, was a descendant of Ruth.

It is faith that is put to the test in the story of Job. To prove to Satan that Job is "a blameless and upright man, who fears God and turns away from evil" (Job 1:8), God heaps misfortune and despair on the luckless man. Through it all, Job remains faithful.

It was that same type of faith that, in the end, would save the Jews from extinction at every turn of their history.

Mishnah: The Six Orders

Jewish belief has never been a fixed creed. Over time generations of Jewish sages and rabbis worked to interpret the Torah and find new meaning within its oral and written texts. For centuries the rabbis resisted writing down the Oral Torah. They wanted students to have to memorize the unwritten laws, because that led to strong bonds between the students and their teachers. But in 132 C.E. the Jews rose up again in revolt against the Romans. So many learned teachers and rabbis were killed that Rabbi Judah ha-Nasi, or Judah the Prince, feared that the Oral Torah might be forgotten forever. Around 200 C.E. he and other scholars began writing down the Oral Torah in a collection called the Mishnah.

Rabbi Judah systematically organized the laws of the Oral Torah into six volumes, or Orders. The Orders covered the laws for farming and prayer; for observing the holy days; for marriage and divorce; for business, ethics, and criminal law; for Temple sacrifice and worship; and for cleanliness and holiness.

While most of the Mishnah is rather dry reading, the section called Pirkei Avot, or "Ethics of the Fathers," includes the moral teachings and proverbs of sixty Jewish teachers. Their wisdom and humor allow readers a glimpse into the rabbinical mind. Modern scholars have added their commentaries to these sayings, which today are a part of everyday life for Jews and non-Jews alike.

The biblical story of Ruth illustrates the virtue of loyalty. Naomi, a Jewish woman, loses her husband and two sons. When the widow decides to settle in Judah, Ruth, her gentile daughter-in-law, begs to go with her, saying, "Your people shall be my people, and your God my God" (Ruth 1:16).

Rabbi Ben Zoma, for example, said, "Who is wise? He who learns learns from every man." Rabbi Meir advised his students to "Look not at the bottle, but at what is in it." The great Pharisee sage Hillel, who lived around 34 B.C.E., asked three famous questions that say much about Jewish belief:

> *If I am not for myself, who will be for me?*
> *If I am only for myself, what am I?*
> *And if not now, when?*

> (Avot 1:14)

Talmud: The Way of the Scholar

The Mishnah became the textbook for generations of rabbis. But, as they had with the Torah, the rabbis felt that the Mishnah needed further interpretation and commentary. In Palestine explanations of the laws in the Mishnah were compiled into the Gemara (from the Aramaic word for "learning" or "completion"). This was completed in 297 C.E. by Rabbi Yohanan bar Nappaha. Rabbi Judah's Mishnah and the Gemara together became known as the Palestinian Talmud, or "teaching."

Between 200 and 500 C.E., the Jews in Babylonia also produced an

AKIVA'S WISDOM

Jewish folklore includes hundreds of stories about rabbis. As a young man Akiva was an illiterate shepherd who went to school with little children to learn the alphabet. He became one of the greatest of Jewish scholars. Around 134 C.E. he was arrested and tortured to death by the Romans.

One day, so a story about him goes, Akiva rode his donkey to a town where he wished to stay the night, but he was refused lodgings. He said, "Everything that God does is for the best," and lay down in a field to sleep. He lit a candle for light and hugged his rooster for warmth.

In the night the wind blew out the candle, a cat ate the rooster, and a lion killed the donkey. Later that night a great army passed by Akiva's field and killed most of the town's inhabitants. "Had they let me stay in the town, I, too, would have been killed!" Akiva exclaimed. "Had my candle been lit, had my rooster crowed, or had my donkey brayed as the army passed, that, too, would have been my end! Truly, everything that God does is for the best."

In this page from a fifteenth-century Italian Hebrew manuscript, butchers slaughter chickens and oxen according to the kosher laws. Animals must be killed swiftly, with one clean stroke of the knife.

enormous Talmud, which includes some of the Palestinian teachings. The Talmud is basically a series of dialogues between rabbis who argue, discuss, and interpret the Mishnah and the Tanakh. It includes some of the Halakhah ("the way of walking, or of behaving"), which deal with the laws of ethical and ritual matters; and some Aggadah ("telling"), which are folktales, parables, legends, the lives of the rabbis, and many teachings on astronomy, logic, medicine, and other sciences. The Talmud also includes detailed laws on every conceivable aspect of daily life and behavior, including birth and death; marriage and marital relations; murder and justice; the correct attitudes toward women and children, parents and neighbors; charity, forgiveness, and hospitality; and the ritual slaughter of animals and the preparation of kosher* food.

The Talmud was originally learned by heart and passed down orally. In the fifth century C.E. the sage Ashi and other scholars began the laborious task of writing it all down. The Talmud contains about 2.5 million words covering more than 15,000 pages.

*Kosher laws decree that animals may not be hunted and that all meat-eating birds and animals are forbidden as food. Only beasts with cloven hooves that regurgitate their meals, such as cows and sheep, are permitted. Animals must be killed with one swift, clean stroke of a knife to avoid bloodshed as much as possible. Many other laws govern the ritual slaughter and cooking of food.

Midrash: Reading between the Lines

The Talmud does not deal with Jewish history. This has been left to the Torah. But generations of rabbis believed that the history of their people as well as their oral and written laws needed to be simplified for the general public. Thus sages including Hillel, his sons, and his students wrote down their midrashim, or "meditations," on the ancient biblical legends. These writings were a kind of "reading between the lines" of the Torah. In them the rabbis invented stories to explain puzzling passages in the biblical legends. In this way they provided a body of popular literature that appealed to young and old alike.

One midrash, for example, explains why Abraham had to leave Ur and portrays him as a young man consumed by religious doubt. It says that Abraham was the son of an idol maker. One day his father, Terah, came home and saw that all the idols had been smashed except the largest, which held an ax in its hand. Abraham told his father that the large idol had smashed all the others.

"You know that these idols cannot move!" shouted Terah.

"If they can't save themselves," Abraham answered, "then we are superior to them, so why should we worship them?"

As the Israelites became dispersed over a huge geographical area, many had no access to learned scholars who could answer their questions about how to conduct their everyday lives. Thus they sent their questions overland to the great schools in Babylonia and Palestine. The rabbis there would ponder the question and eventually return an answer, known as a responsum. This answer was sent to all the centers of learning so that all Jews received the same reply to the question. Today there is no universal center of Jewish learning, but people still send questions to their rabbis and expect responsa in return.

Over the centuries the responsa offer a fascinating mirror of changing times. Five hundred years ago a question might have involved the correct way in which to slaughter an animal. Today practicing Jews want to know the answers to questions such as whether it is permissible to drive to a service on the Sabbath, when work of any kind—including driving—is forbidden.

Opposite: *Nearly two thousand years after the Talmud was written, scholars continue to analyze and debate Jewish law. Arguing fine points of logic helps train the mind of the scholar. This painting of Talmudists, by Max Weber, was completed in 1934.*

CHAPTER FOUR

THE UNIVERSAL WAY

By the fifth century B.C.E., following the end of the Babylonian exile, many Jews had settled in Ethiopia and as far away as India and even China. Their dispersal all over the known world is called the Diaspora, from the Greek word for "scattering."

The Torah and, later, the Talmud gave Jews a blueprint for survival in exile, far from the Promised Land. They believed that whatever happened to them was the work of God, and not of mortal kings and conquerors. Many were convinced that if they were persecuted or banished, it was because they had been less than perfect in God's eyes. If they worked toward righteousness and goodness, then God would surely forgive them and lead them back to the Promised Land. Though this might take centuries, the Jews were prepared to wait.

The Jews practiced many professions and were particularly renowned as merchants and physicians. Because they were literate, they often became court advisers to kings and emperors. Yet they never forgot their Covenant. While other nations strove to conquer territory, the Jews strove for knowledge and wisdom. While others built armies of soldiers, the Jews built armies of scholars.

Centers of Learning

Babylonia

In Babylonia the exiled Jews were tolerated by a series of Babylonian, Persian, Greek, and Roman rulers. For some eight hundred years the exiles prospered there, especially in the city of Babylon. Their political leader, or head of state, was called the *exilarch*, or "prince of the Diaspora." He usually lived in great splendor, almost like a king. Among other duties, the *exilarch* collected taxes and appointed judges. The Jews' spiritual leaders were known as *gaon* (GAH-on). They were selected from three famous schools, or yeshivas, in the cities of Sura, Pumpaditha, and Nehardea. These great academies had the same standing then that

A Jewish scholar at work in his study during the Middle Ages

Oxford University in England or the Ivy League universities in the United States enjoy today.

It was in the Babylonian yeshivas that the Talmud was compiled and the tradition of Talmudic learning was begun. Among the Jews, learning and intellectual pursuits had become the highest priorities. When a king died, any suitable person could replace him. When a scholar died, no one could replace him.

Alexandria

The Jews had little influence over most peoples among whom they lived. But when the Greeks conquered the Persian Empire in 332 B.C.E., the result was a dynamic fusion of Greek and Jewish thought. This was centered in two great cities: Jerusalem, which had flowered again, and Alexandria, which Alexander the Great founded on the Mediterranean coast of Egypt.

The Greeks built Alexandria on a lavish scale. Because the city was located on the sea routes between Europe and Asia, its markets boasted international goods from Arabian spices to East African ivory. Alexandria was graced with spacious temples, well-planned streets, and luxurious bathhouses. There was a fine museum with lecture halls, laboratories, and a zoo, as well as a library with thousands of scrolls that contained all the available knowledge of the time. Most magnificent of all was the Pharos, a lighthouse soaring 440 feet (134 meters) into the air. The Pharos was considered one of the Seven Wonders of the World.

Many Jews arrived in Alexandria as deportees, sent there by various conquerors of Judah. Others came willingly. The Jewish community flourished, and Alexandria gradually replaced the city of Babylon as a center of Jewish learning. By about 250 B.C.E. Alexandrian Jews had become so hellenized, or influenced by Greek culture, that their leaders ordered a translation of the Hebrew Tanakh into Greek. Legend has it that seventy scholars each completed an independent translation. When compared, the

Opposite: *The Pharos was designed by the Greek architect Sostratus and was built during the reign of Ptolemy II (283–246 B.C.E.). A fire at the top guided ships into Alexandria for 1,500 years before the magnificent lighthouse was destroyed by an earthquake. No one knows what the Pharos really looked like, but many artists have based their reconstructions on eyewitness reports.*

versions were identical—a sign that God's hand had guided the work. This Bible became known as the Septuagint, or the "Book of the Seventy."

The Septuagint became a best-seller. It fulfilled its purpose, drawing hellenized Jews back to traditional Judaism. It also affected the entire Greek-speaking world. Pagans, who worshipped many gods, were fascinated by the idea of one God; by Jewish humanitarianism, especially toward slaves; and by the Sabbath, a holy day off from work. During the first and second centuries B.C.E. many non-Jews converted to Judaism. Later most of the New Testament, or Christian Bible, was first written in Greek by the Greek-speaking Jews who founded Christianity.

Yavneh

Alexandria remained the center of Jewish intellectual life from about 200 B.C.E. to 100 C.E. As the Romans grew in power and eventually conquered the Greek empire, however, this flame slowly died. The scene shifted back to the Jewish community in Judah, or Judea, as it was called by the Romans.

In 68 C.E. Jerusalem was under siege by the Romans. Among the Pharisee rabbis trapped inside the city was Yohanan ben Zakkai, a great scholar and a former student of the sage Hillel. Yohanan could not save Jerusalem, but he was determined to save the rabbis, who had centuries of Hebrew history and wisdom at their fingertips. Hidden in a coffin, Yohanan escaped from the city to confront the Roman general Vespasian. The scholar's courage paid off. Vespasian granted Yohanan permission to found a small yeshiva, or school of Jewish learning, in nearby Yavneh.

At the Temple in Jerusalem the Pharisees had established a supreme court, known as the Sanhedrin. With the Temple gone, Yohanan established a new Sanhedrin at Yavneh. There seventy-one rabbis and scholars met to discuss matters of Jewish politics and religion (the odd number made a tied vote impossible). The Sanhedrin judged all disputes and matters of business and daily life according to the ways of the Torah.

Rabbis and scholars from all over the Diaspora flocked to Yavneh to study. Some of them traveled throughout ravaged Judea, teaching and founding schools. The Torah—once exclusive to the educated priests—became available to everyone, rich and poor, young and old alike. This remarkably progressive idea created literate Jewish communities in regions where almost everyone else was illiterate.

Foundations for the Future

After the fall of Jerusalem in 70 C.E., the Jews continued to resist the Romans but were basically powerless in their own country. The majority of Jews were dispersed over vast areas in the Diaspora. Yohanan ben Zakkai feared that they would forget their Covenant, their laws, and their language. To preserve Judaism forever, he and his pupils developed codes of conduct that would unite Jews and help them to survive wherever they lived. When Yohanan died around 80 C.E., his successors in Yavneh continued his work. The laws they enacted were dispersed throughout the Diaspora, and some remain in force today.

MONOTHEISM: ONE IDEA, THREE VOICES

When Palestine was under Roman rule, Jesus Christ made a name for himself as a Jewish teacher. Though he obeyed the Torah, some of his teachings differed greatly from its laws. Jesus taught that he was the Son of God, that he had the power to forgive all sins, and that people could only know God through him. The Jews had long believed in the coming of the Messiah or, in Greek, the Christ. The Messiah would be a military leader who would free the Jews from persecution and usher in a new age of peace. Jesus' followers believed that he was the Messiah. In Roman eyes this was reason enough for his crucifixion in 33 C.E.

After Jesus' death Paul, an early believer in him, had a vision in which he saw Jesus as God. This led Paul to believe that what God wanted was not observance of the Torah but faith in Jesus. He preached that Jesus had died in order to atone for humankind's sins and thus added new spiritual meaning to the word *Messiah*. The followers of Paul's teachings came to be called Christians. At this point Christianity separated from traditional Judaism and became a religion of its own. This new faith was attractive to many pagans, mainly because it offered a promise of life after death. In 313 C.E. Christianity was accepted as the official religion of the Roman Empire. This acceptance was accompanied by a deep rejection of those Jews who continued to follow the old faith. As Christianity spread throughout Europe, hatred of Jews became firmly rooted in the West.

Muhammad, who founded Islam in 610 C.E., was familiar with Judaism and with Christianity. He called himself the Prophet, last in the line of prophets that included Adam, Noah, Abraham, Moses, Solomon, and Jesus. Muhammad claimed that his was the last true message from the One God, Allah, who was the same god as the Elohim worshipped by the Jews. Neither Jews nor Christians accepted Muhammad as a prophet, nor did they accept the Koran, his holy book.

To prevent the Hebrew language from disappearing, the Yavneh scholars compiled the first Hebrew dictionary and grammar. To ensure that Jews worshiped in the same way, the Jewish prayers and services were published and distributed to synagogues everywhere. Torah readings in the synagogues were no longer restricted to specialists; any adult male member of the community could read publicly from the scroll.

Under the new laws, any time 10 Jewish males over the age of thirteen lived near one another, they had to establish a religious community, or kahal, and build a synagogue. If there were 120 or more males, they could establish a social community and their own local court. The court supervised all social and commercial functions. It specified wages and prices, for example, and oversaw the ritual slaughtering of meat.

One of the most important of the Yavneh laws stipulated that every Jew was "his brother's keeper." Thus, when a Jew was taken into slavery, the nearest Jewish community was obliged to buy his freedom within seven years.

Eventually most Jewish communities expanded. They built libraries and schools, rooms for visitors, houses for ritual baths, funeral facilities, courtrooms, and community centers where marriages and other festivals were celebrated. In some cities, such as Alexandria, the Jewish quarters were magnificent. In other places such communities remained modest, even poor.

Within Jewish communities schooling for boys was required by law, and girls could attend if they wished. Tuition was free to the fatherless, to orphans, and to the poor. Good salaries were paid to attract highly qualified people to teaching.

The Jewish marriage contract, like this seventeenth-century example, outlines a husband and wife's duties toward each other.

No one—not even non-Jews—was allowed to go hungry or homeless. The Jews imposed taxes on their communities to pay for charity and education. This way they needed no support from their foreign governments.

The genius of the Yavneh scholars came most vividly to life in the laws they enacted to promote good relations with other peoples in the Diaspora. For example, Jews in foreign countries had to recognize the validity of non-Jewish documents in any court and of all non-Jewish oaths made in any country, in any language. Jews also had to obey the laws of their host country, as long as these did not forbid their religious practices. Finally, in times of war the Jews had to defend the country they inhabited, even if this meant fighting against other Jews.

The Jewish community was responsible for burying its dead, and belonging to a burial society was a great honor. This seventeenth-century painting shows a burial ceremony in Venice.

Feasts and Festivals

Most Jewish holidays celebrate historical events. The Hebrew calendar is a lunar one, based on the cycles of the moon. A year has 354 days instead of the 365 days of the solar calendar. A complete

IF YOU LIVED IN ANCIENT JUDEA

If you had been born in Judea during the first century B.C.E., you would have witnessed the decline of Greek influence there, followed by the rise of Roman power. With this chart you can trace the course your life might have taken as a member of an ordinary Jewish farming family.

You were born in Judea. . . .

As a Boy . . .   As a Girl . . .

You live in a village in a house made of stone or brick. Wooden beams support a flat, plastered roof. The house includes several bedrooms and storerooms, a kitchen, a living room, and an interior courtyard. Your father, mother, brothers, sisters, several slaves, and your father's other wives and concubines may all live with you. Your family may grow olive trees, various grains, and fruits and vegetables, and raise cattle and honeybees.

At age 8 days you are named and circumcised in the synagogue.

▼

At about age 7 you attend a school where you learn to read the Scriptures in Hebrew. At home you speak both Hebrew and Aramaic and possibly Greek. You take care of your family's farm animals and crops.

▼

At age 13 you take some adult responsibilities and must perform *aliyah*—reading from the Torah in the synagogue. (This initiation will later become known as *bar mitzvah*, when a boy becomes a "son of the commandments" and must obey Jewish laws.)

▼

As a young man you continue to work your father's farm. When you are in your late teens or early twenties, your father seeks a bride for you. Your marriage plans must be announced a full year before the wedding. You give your wife a marriage contract and promise to support her. If you can afford them, you add concubines to your family. If you divorce, you must pay alimony. You and your family live with or close to your parents.

Until about age 10 you learn cooking, sewing, and other household skills from your mother and other women in the house. You speak Hebrew, Aramaic, and possibly Greek. You do not attend school.

▼

After you reach age 11 your father is duty-bound to find a groom for you. You spend the year after the wedding announcement preparing for married life.

▼

As a wife you live with or near your husband's parents. You are expected to obey your husband, provide him with sons, manage the household, help the needy, make and sell linen garments, and care for your family's gardens, vineyards, and domestic animals. You may be one of many wives and concubines and can be divorced against your will. If you are widowed, the Jewish community will help you.

When you die, a burial society of men for males and women for females prepares your body by ritually cleaning it. For seven days after the funeral, your closest relatives stay at home to symbolize their sad feelings.

cycle takes nineteen years, and for seven of those years an extra month is added so that the official holidays fall at the correct time of year. New holidays, such as Israeli Independence Day, are added as the course of Jewish history continues.

Days of Atonement:
September/October—Tishri 1 and 2 to 10

The seventh month of the Hebrew calendar, known as Nisan, occurs during March/April. But Jews celebrate their New Year, or Rosh Hashanah, during September/October, in the month of Tishri. They believe that Tishri is when God created the world. The period between Rosh Hashanah and Yom Kippur, or the "Day of Atonement," which occurs ten days later, is known as the High Holy Days and deals literally with matters of life and death. During this time Jews must carefully examine their personal lives and their consciences, and confess their sins, in order to redeem themselves before God. They believe that between Rosh Hashanah and Yom Kippur God decides "how many shall leave this world, and how many shall be born into it, who shall live and who shall die . . . who shall be at peace and who shall be tormented" (from the *Machzor*, a traditional liturgy for this holiday).

Sukkot:
September/October—Tishri

Sukkot, or the Festival of Booths, celebrates the fall harvest. A simple structure called a sukkah is built outdoors of branches or boughs. It must be open to the sky, so that the stars can be seen at night. The sukkah is decorated with fruit, vegetables, and other foods harvested at this time of year. Each day for eight days, families or groups of people eat at least one meal in the sukkah. As a form of blessing, participants shake a sheaf made of seven different plant species and one kind of citrus fruit over one another.

Hanukkah:
November/December—Kislev 25

Hanukkah is a joyous festival commemorating the reestablishment of the Temple in Jerusalem by the Maccabees in 164 B.C.E. To satisfy ritual needs during the rededication, oil had to be burned for eight days, but only enough could be found for one day. According to Jewish tradition, that oil miraculously lasted for the required eight. Hannukah thus is celebrated for eight days, symbolized by eight candles held in a special candleholder called a menorah. A ninth candle is used to light one candle each day.

Purim:
February/March—Adar 14
This delightful festival celebrates the actions of the biblical Esther. She married the king of Persia but hid her Jewish heritage from him. When the king was persuaded by his evil adviser, Haman, to wipe out the Jews, Esther followed her cousin Mordecai's advice and risked her life to change her husband's mind. She succeeded, and Haman was hanged.

At Purim Jewish men and women listen to a public reading of the scroll of Esther. They often come in fancy dress, carrying noisemakers called *groggers*. Whenever the name of Haman is mentioned—which occurs more than fifty times during the reading—people hiss, boo, yell, and rattle their *groggers*. On the serious side, at Purim Jews are expected to send gifts of food and drink to other Jews and to honor requests for charity. Jewish communities throughout the world establish their own Purim celebrations to commemorate times when they were saved from destruction at the hands of anti-Semites.

Passover:
March/April—Nisan 15 to 22
Passover is the most widely observed Jewish holiday. During Moses' time, the Bible says, the last of the ten plagues that God inflicted on the Egyptians was the death of every firstborn Egyptian child. The day before the killing Moses had the Israelites sprinkle lamb's blood on their doorposts. This way the Angel of Death would know which houses were occupied by Israelites and would *pass over* them. When the pharaoh finally allowed the Israelites to leave Egypt, they departed in such a hurry that there was no time for their bread to rise. They took with them the flat bread known as matzo.

At the Passover seder, or feast, Jews eat matzo, as well as *maror*, a bitter herb (usually fresh horseradish) symbolizing the bitterness of Jewish slavery in Egypt, and *kharoset*, a mixture of crushed nuts and apples representing the mortar that Hebrew slaves manufactured for their

Oil is poured into the branches of a menorah and kept burning for eight days to celebrate Hanukkah. Today candles are used.

Egyptian masters. Four cups of wine are drunk. The fifth—Elijah's cup—is left untouched in the belief that the prophet Elijah visits every seder to drink from his cup. To learn about the Exodus, children listen to the Haggadah, a story outlining the liberation of the Israelites from Egypt.

CHAPTER FIVE

PAST, PRESENT, AND FUTURE

During the exile in Babylonia, most Jews prospered. After Cyrus the Great granted Jews their freedom in 538 B.C.E., only about 40,000 chose to return to Judah. The majority elected to stay in Babylonia. In time they built communities throughout the Persian Empire. The Greek and Roman conquests brought Jews into cities in western Europe (in what are now Italy, France, and southern Germany). As the Middle Ages progressed, the Jews established themselves farther north, in England, northern Germany, Belgium, Holland, Scandinavia, Poland, and Russia. These Jews came to be known as Ashkenazim (ahsh-kuh-NAH-zuhm), after Ashkenaz, the Hebrew name for Germany.

Meanwhile, after the founding of Islam in the seventh century C.E., the Middle Ages saw the rise and golden age of the Muslim empire. From the ninth to midthirteenth centuries, that empire encompassed a territory stretching from India in the east to Spain in the west. It included most of northern Africa as well as lands such as Palestine and Persia, which had previously belonged to the Persian, Greek, and Roman empires. The majority of Jews had settled in these areas, and they now found themselves under Muslim rule. In time the Jews of Spain and the Arab world came to be known as Sephardim, after Sepharadh, the Hebrew word for Spain.

Like the Jews, the Muslims believed in only one God, Allah. (Allah is the Arabic word for God.) In his name they had waged holy war to win new territories for Islam. Pagan nonbelievers were not tolerated. However, the first Muslims realized that Jews played a vital role in the economy of most of the conquered territories, especially in the large cities. Muslims also respected Jews and Christians as "people of the book" and cobelievers in the One God and therefore awarded them the status of *ahl al-dhimma*, or "the protected people." This meant that as

Opposite: *Europe's oldest synagogue is in Prague, the capital of the Czech Republic, and dates back to the thirteenth century.*

long as *dhimmis* paid poll and land taxes, their lives and property were protected and they had freedom of faith and worship.

Dhimmis did not live as equal citizens with Muslims. Many restrictions were imposed specifically to remind them of their lowly status. For example, they could ride only donkeys, not horses or mules, and they always had to give way to a Muslim. During some periods they had to wear ridiculous clothes or a ball around the neck. In 1146, when a fanatical sect came to power, Jews in Fez, Morocco, were offered Islam or the sword, and most were murdered. On the whole, however, Jews enjoyed more freedom under Muslim rule than they did under the Christians.

Trade: A Tool for Survival

Ancient Babylonia was a vital pivot for trade between the Far East, the Middle East, and the West. Thus, while Jews in Babylonia were free to practice many professions, the vast majority of them were merchant traders. They used routes already established by Arab and Indian traders. When the Muslims conquered the Middle East, Jews became the middlemen between the Christian West, the Muslim empire, and the Far East.

Jewish merchants made extraordinary journeys to the far corners of the known world. They traveled thousands of miles by land and sea, establishing synagogues and small Jewish communities along trade routes that stretched from China to England, from Scandinavia to Egypt. From the nomadic shepherds of northern Russia, the Jews bought wool and lamb's fur, which they traded with Vikings for precious ambergris (an important ingredient of perfume), gold ornaments, and salted fish, a favorite food throughout Europe and the Middle East. This trade with the north was so important to both Jewish and Arab traders that during the twelfth and thirteenth centuries more Arab than native coins circulated in the Scandinavian countries! From western and southern Europe, Jewish traders brought silver, textiles, and various grains to northern Europe. From the Arab countries came leather and metalware. Gold, silver, grains, furs, textiles, and a variety of leather and metal goods were exchanged for exotic silks, perfumes, jewels, pearls, spices, and porcelain from China and India.

For centuries Jews in Europe conducted their business in peace and prospered. But during the Middle Ages, when the Catholic Church was the dominant power in Europe, Christian anti-Semitism eventually brought Jewish trade to a standstill. Jewish ships were pirated and sunk,

This medieval stained glass window shows Jews in their many professions, including astronomer, banker, translator, architect, pharmacist, and wine merchant.

and trade routes to the Far East were taken over by their rivals, the Venetians. By the fifteenth century the bulk of Jewish trading in the Diaspora was over.

In the Arab World

Within the Islamic empire, Arabic became the common language. It also became the main language of scholarship among the Jews, who wrote it using Hebrew characters.

The first center of Jewish learning in the Arab world was Baghdad. Arabs had rediscovered and added to the philosophical, scientific, and literary works of the ancient Greeks. Several

Jewish scholars undertook the task of translating these works—especially the medical treatises—into Arabic.

It was in Muslim Spain, or Andalusia, from the tenth to twelfth centuries, that the interaction between Hebrew culture and Arab/Islamic civilization arrived at its golden age. Wealthy Jews in great cities such as Granada and Cordoba lived in palatial splendor, as described in a poem by Solomon ibn Gabirol:

> *A palace rose above the countryside*
> *Built with valiant stones*
> *Its walls thick as battlements*
> *With balconies around*
> *The buildings decked with reliefs*
> *Laid out with alabaster floors*
> *Windows shining from above*
> *The countless gates and ivory doors.**

Maimonides' signature accompanies this twelfth-century portrait of the famous philosopher.

Jewish writers in Andalusia produced major works of theology, science, philosophy, and literature, and new studies of the Torah and the Talmud flourished. Hisdai ibn Shaprut, for example, translated a huge botanical work from Greek into Arabic. This was also the age of great Jewish poets such as Samuel Hanagid, Moses ibn Ezra, and Judah Halevi. They adapted Arabic rhythms to their Hebrew poems on love, friendship, war, and nature and composed hymns to God. Other authors wrote scholarly comparisons of Judaism to other religions.

This period came to an abrupt end in 1147, when the Almohads, a fanatical Muslim sect, came to power in Spain. Jews who refused to convert to Islam were forced to flee. Among them was Moses ben Maimon, known as Maimonides (my-MAHN-ih-deez), recognized as the most influential Jewish thinker of the Middle Ages, if not of all time. Maimonides fled to Cairo, where he became physician to the sultan of Egypt. His major work was the fourteen-volume *Mishneh Torah*. Together with the Torah, Maimonides' book provided rules for behavior on all occasions, freeing Jews from having to search through the Talmud for guidelines. Though it raised much controversy at the

*From *The Jews: Story of a People*, Howard Fast (New York: Dial Press, 1968)

PHYSICIANS TO THE WORLD

From very ancient times Jewish specialists performed dissections of human and animal bodies. They had excellent surgical tools for operations such as circumcision and cesarean section (surgery for childbirth) and for the suturing (sewing) of severed veins and arteries. Through their international connections, Jews obtained drugs to reduce pain, cause unconsciousness during surgery, and heal wounds.

Jewish butchers noticed that external symptoms of disease were often related to internal problems. With knowledge based on this groundbreaking discovery, the Talmud contains lengthy discussions on the functions and diseases of the liver, lungs, heart, brain, and most other internal and external organs.

While Christian nations still foundered in superstition and illiteracy, Jewish doctors became physicians to Christian and Muslim, to poor and rich. Far too valuable to lose, doctors were often spared in anti-Semitic attacks. Jewish doctors today follow in the footsteps of their forebears and are equally prominent.

time, the *Mishneh Torah* is studied to this day by yeshiva students. Maimonides' major philosophical work was *The Guide to the Perplexed*, an explanation of puzzling passages in the Bible.

Meanwhile, Europe had begun to discover Arabic learning. In 1085 Spanish Christian armies conquered the city of Toledo. The valuable manuscripts in the city's many libraries and schools became available to Christian scholars, who founded a school for translation in Toledo. Once again Jews played a major role in this transfer of knowledge. They translated Arabic texts on medicine, architecture, astronomy, astrology, physics, magic, mathematics, and philosophy into Latin, Spanish, and French. They renewed Hebrew as their language of science. In many fields they provided texts that form the basis of modern knowledge.

The Seeds Are Sown

The Jews have always had to fight for their religious and political freedom. Their belief in one God often caused conflict between the early Hebrews and surrounding pagans. Their conviction that they are God's Chosen People, here to perfect the world in his eyes, also set them apart from others and caused resentment.

Christians condemned Jews for "killing" Christ, himself a Jew, because his disciple Judas Iscariot—also a Jew—delivered him to the Romans for crucifixion. Christians also condemned Jews for rejecting Jesus as the Messiah.

During the Middle Ages Christians accused Jews of committing "blood libel"—of murdering non-Jews in religious rituals and using their blood to bake matzo. Idiotic claims such as these resurfaced throughout history. From 1347 to 1353, for example, the Black Death, a flea-and-rat-borne plague, swept Europe, killing off two-thirds of the population. This raised hysterical claims that Jews had poisoned wells to start the plague and kill off Christians. Jews were slaughtered in untold numbers.

The Seeds Bear Fruit

Culture in the Muslim world of the Middle Ages was far more advanced and sophisticated than in the West. People in North Africa and the Near East were used to foreign travelers, and the cosmopolitan Jews were at home in the most magnificent courts and busiest marketplaces of the time. Learning was centered in the Arab world, and Jews there were a vital link in the exchange of information and ideas. In western Europe, however, the learned, peace-loving Jews stood out in an almost entirely Christian, constantly warring society. Most Europeans were illiterate and held primitive views about the rest of the world. With the encouragement of the Christian Church, they made Jews a target for their hatred and bigotry.

Starting in 1096, Christian knights and common folk by the thousands marched through Europe on the Crusades to deliver the Holy Land from the Muslims. On the way they wiped out entire Jewish communities, massacring Jews as vengeance "for the blood of Christ."

One after the other, England, Spain, and most other European nations expelled the Jews, forcing them to flee. Some Jews found new homes in North Africa, Greece, and Turkey. A few came to the New World of the Americas. Many scurried north to Poland, where they flowered briefly before anti-Semitism caught up with them.

Often the Talmud was publicly burned. In the cities Jews had often built their communities in walled areas known as ghettos. Now they were confined to ghettos by law and could be expelled from them at any time. They were heavily taxed, forbidden to own land or join craft guilds, and barred from most professions. Only their experience in international trade and finance saved them, for over the years they had proven invaluable to gentiles (non-Jews) as tax collectors, estate administrators, and money-lenders. In some regions the Jews had become essential to the economy. Though they were permitted to lend money and were sorely needed for this service, since the Church forbade Christians from doing so, they were also bitterly hated for providing it.

From the fifteenth to seventeenth centuries the Renaissance in western Europe brought greater tolerance for the Jews. The French Revolution, which began in 1789, brought equal rights to all citizens of France, including the Jews. Other nations soon followed suit. While many old laws remained active, Jews could study in universities and follow most professions. Their numbers increased, and many reached prominent positions in all walks of life.

Nevertheless, the old hatreds continued to resurface. Prejudice against Jews was no longer purely religious. It had become political and racial as well. By the nineteenth century more than half of the world's Jews lived in Russia. Thousands were mercilessly slaughtered in three vicious attacks, or pogroms. Millions

Survivors of a pogrom. Painted in 1910 by Polish artist Maurycy Minkowski.

emigrated to the United States, Canada, South Africa, and Australia. In the 1940s, during Adolf Hitler's Holocaust, six million Jews were murdered. This sent a second wave of refugees to South America, Africa, and the United States, and provided the final impetus for the establishment of the state of Israel.

In many countries of the world Jews today live in relative peace. Yet, like a snake that will not die, anti-Semitism continues to rear its ugly head from time to time.

The Nation of Israel

If I forget thee, O Jerusalem
Let my right hand wither. . . .

Psalm 137, written during the Babylonian exile, shows the extraordinary connection Jews felt to the Promised Land. They firmly believed that God would one day lead them back there. The terrible pogroms in Russia during the late 1800s, however, convinced many Jews that it was time to take matters into their own hands and escape to Palestine, or Zion*, as it was called. In 1882 the first Russian Zionists emigrated to Palestine. They were soon followed by thousands more. Funded by wealthy Jews in other nations, the Zionists bought Arab lands and began to develop them. In 1914 World War I broke out, and Palestine and the rest of the Middle East became a battleground. By the end of 1917 the British had occupied Jerusalem and proclaimed their support for a Jewish homeland in Palestine.

Unfortunately, Arab families had been living in Palestine for many generations and already had economic and spiritual claims to the land. They believed that Muhammad had taken his first steps to heaven from Jerusalem. For this and many other reasons, Arabs claimed Jerusalem as a holy city of Islam, second only to Mecca, their holy city near the Red Sea.

From the start Jews and Arabs in Palestine were thrown into bitter conflict. The Holocaust increased the pressure to find a new homeland for millions of Jews. Many places, including Kenya and Uganda, were sug-

---

*When King David captured Jerusalem from the Canaanite Jebusites, the city's main citadel was called Zion. The name came to stand for the city of Jerusalem and for the Jewish homeland.

gested, but the Zionists would accept only their ancient Holy Land as a site for the modern state of Israel. In 1947 the United Nations proposed a solution. Under its Partition Plan, Palestine would be carved in two: part of the land for the Jews, part for the Palestinian Arabs.

Jews all over the world rejoiced, but Arabs everywhere rejected the proposal. They were not against Jews living among them—they always had—but they believed that the Partition Plan divided the land unfairly. Despite Arab resistance, however, the plan was passed by the world powers. On May 14, 1948, the modern state of Israel was born.

About 20,000 Zionist immigrants arrived in Palestine between 1906 and 1914. Most were young people who had witnessed the terrible pogroms in Russia. Many were students or the sons of middle-class families, but in their new homeland, they became farmers.

The next day the five surrounding Arab nations launched an attack. In the war that followed, Israel defeated the Arab forces, who were poorly armed and trained. Ever since, war after war has pitted Israelis and Arabs against each other. Despite several attempts at making peace, the conflicts begun in biblical times continue.

A Palestinian argues with Israeli soldiers in Jerusalem. Violent conflicts have flared again and again in the region since the establishment of the modern state of Israel.

The Intellectual Legacy

The late nineteenth and early twentieth centuries were a period of enlightenment for all western Europe and the United States. Three German Jews led the field: Karl Marx founded modern communism, Sigmund Freud founded modern psychology, and Albert Einstein developed his theory of relativity. Their names will resound through history forever.

There are hundreds of other Jews who made major discov-

FOUR BRANCHES OF THE TREE

In 1840, in an attempt to modernize Jewish practices, Abraham Geiger and Samuel Holdheim founded Reform Judaism. They argued that the Jews are not a separate people but rather a union of many peoples who follow Judaism. To Geiger and Holdheim the ancient customs and rituals of the Talmud were no longer relevant. Instead they focused on the moral teachings of the prophets, which would be "a lamp unto the nations," guiding others in ethical behavior.

In response to Reform Judaism, the German rabbi Samson Raphael Hirsch founded Neo- or New Orthodoxy. Hirsch insisted on following the laws of the Talmud. But unlike Orthodox Jews, he allowed nonreligious studies and delivered his sermons in German instead of Hebrew.

Conservative Judaism was founded by Zechariah Frankel. He wanted to "conserve" the Jewish past by keeping old laws that were still useful but replacing outdated ones with new ones as needed.

In the 1940s Mordecai Kaplan founded the Reconstructionist Movement in the United States. Kaplan rejected the idea of one all-knowing God and the ancient belief that the Jews are God's Chosen People. Instead he believed that the spirit of God lives within each person, guiding the conscience. Despite their differences, the four branches of thought, together with the traditional Orthodox root, are united in preserving the future of Judaism.

eries in mathematics, chemistry, physics, astronomy, and medicine. Their work ranged from the discovery of disease-bearing microorganisms to the idea of nuclear fission in atomic energy. In politics Jews held prominent posts in nearly every court and cabinet. England's prime minister Benjamin Disraeli was a Jew, as was Leon Trotsky, one of the leaders of the Communist Revolution in Russia in 1917. And where once the Jewish moneylender was despised, now great banking families such as the Rothschilds financed huge industrial ventures.

By the early twentieth century, however, renewed persecution had forced millions of Jews to emigrate to the United States, which guaranteed "liberty and justice for all." Where most Jewish immigrants began as poor workers, many soon prospered. Jews served as advisers to presi-

dents, became governors of cities, and presided in court. Their star shone particularly in the field of entertainment. Jews founded the movie industry in the United States, providing many of its finest producers. The genius of Jewish composers such as Richard Rodgers and Oscar Hammerstein II helped create the modern musical comedy. Performers of classical music, including pianist Vladimir Horowitz and violinist Yehudi Menuhin, as well as conductors such as Leonard Bernstein will never be forgotten. The movies of Danny Kaye, the Marx Brothers, and other Jewish comedians have brought laughter to worldwide audiences.

Today American Jews continue to contribute to cultural and political life in the United States and abroad. Richard Feynman's theory of ordered chaos has inspired new directions in scientific research. Woody Allen and Steven Spielberg, to name but a couple, are among the most famous filmmakers. Actors such as Dustin Hoffman and Bette Midler enjoy international renown. Folksinger Bob Dylan influenced an entire generation of young political activists, while authors including Saul Bellow and Isaac Bashevis Singer have produced some of the twentieth century's finest works of literature. Henry Kissinger, former secretary of state, influenced world politics for several decades. Throughout the world Jewish contributions to science and technology are particularly valued, and more Jews than any other people have won the Nobel Prize.

Perhaps the Jews' extraordinary success in so many fields can be traced back to centuries of scholarship and debate on the Torah and the Talmud. These works deal not only with the details of Judaism but with basic human issues of social justice and morality. No wonder, then, that Jews continue to probe the mysteries of the human condition by every possible means.

Opposite: *A man holds the Torah in this dreamlike painting by the famous Jewish artist Marc Chagall (1887–1985). Chagall was born in Russia but painted mainly in France.*

The Ancient Hebrews: A Time Line

B.C.E.

19th–16th centuries
Abraham leaves Ur and enters Canaan

12th and 11th centuries
Period of judges

9th–6th centuries
The age of prophets

2000   1500   1000   500   100

1650
The Hyksos conquer Egypt

1279–1212
Reign of Pharaoh Ramses II

1220
Death of Moses

1004–965
Reign of David

967–928
Reign of Solomon

967–586
First Temple period

928
Reign of Rehoboam; division of kingdom of Israel into kingdoms of Judah and Israel

722
Kingdom of Israel destroyed by Assyria

586
Judah conquered by Nebuchadrezzar, king of Babylonia; destruction of First Temple; Jewish exile in Babylonia

539
Cyrus, king of Persia, conquers Babylonia

539
Jews from Babylonia return to Judah

539 (to 70 C.E.)
Second Temple period

515
Completion of Second Temple

458
Ezra arrives in Israel

444
It is decreed that the Torah (the Five Books of Moses) may never be added to or changed in any way

332
Alexander the Great conquers Persian Empire

250
Hebrew Bible translated into Greek; called the Septuagint

200 (to 100 C.E.)
Alexandria center of Jewish intellectual activity

175
Judah ruled by Syrian king Antiochus Epiphanes

164
Maccabees reclaim Jerusalem and purify the Temple

63
Judah falls to Romans
c. 6 Birth of Jesus Christ

C.E.

10th–12th centuries
Golden age of Spanish Jewry

100   500   1000   1500   2000

33
Jesus Christ crucified

66
Romans besiege Jerusalem

70
Destruction of
Second Temple by Romans

c. 80
Death of Yohanan
ben Zakkai

200 (to 500)
Compilation of
Babylonian Talmud

297
Completion of
Palestinian Talmud

313
Christianity becomes official
religion of Roman Empire

610
Muhammad founds Islam

1096
First Crusade

1147
Almohads come to power
in Spain

1290
Jews expelled from England

1492
Jews expelled from Spain

1791
French Jews granted
citizenship

1914–1918
World War I

1939–1945
World War II

1948
State of Israel founded

GLOSSARY

Aggadah: parts of the Talmud and the midrash that include folktales, legends, parables, sayings, and other wisdom

'Am Yisrael: "the people of Israel"

anti-Semite: one who hates Jews

Ark of the Covenant: chest, placed in the holiest room of the Temple in Jerusalem, where the stone tablets on which the Ten Commandments were written were kept

Ashkenazim: one of the two great divisions of Jews, made up of the Yiddish-speaking Jews of eastern Europe; see *Sephardim*

Baal: the Canaanite fertility god

bar mitzvah: a Jewish boy who reaches his thirteenth birthday and is thus considered an adult who must obey the laws of the Torah; also, the ceremony recognizing a boy as a bar mitzvah

B'nai Yisrael: "the children of Israel"

Canaanites: members of many different Semitic groups inhabiting Canaan

circumcise: to remove the foreskin of the penis

concubine: a woman who lives with a man without being married

Covenant: the binding contract that Abraham made with God

Diaspora: the scattering of Jews to countries outside Israel

El, El Shaddai: the Hebrew God, "El of the Mountain"

Elohim: Lord; a synonym for "God"

epiphany: an appearance of a divine being to a human

Essenes (ih-SEENS): a Hebrew sect

exile: being forced to live outside one's own country

Exodus: the ancient Hebrews' flight from slavery in Egypt

Gemara: commentaries and rulings on the Mishnah

gentile: a non-Jew

ghetto: a walled-in area of a city in which Jews lived apart from others

Haggadah: the story of the Exodus, recited to children at Passover

Halakhah: Talmudic laws for correct observance of ethics and rituals

Hellenism: Greek culture from 332 B.C.E. to about 30 C.E., as adopted by other peoples

Holocaust: the murder of over six million Jews during World War II

Hyksos (HICK-sohs): an Asiatic people who invaded Egypt around 1650 B.C.E., gaining control of the Nile delta

idol: a painted or carved image of a god or goddess

Israelites: the descendants of the Hebrews

Jehovah: the Hebrew God; also known as Yahweh or JHVH

Judaism: the Jewish belief system

Ketuvim: stories, psalms, and other writings in the Tanakh

liturgy: prayers or a service in a place of worship

matriarch: a scriptural mother of the Hebrew people

matzo: unleavened bread eaten at Passover

menorah: an eight-branched candleholder used during Hanukkah

Messiah: in Jewish theology, a descendant of David who will bring together the Jewish people and usher in an era of peace and harmony

midrash: a rabbinical meditation on the meaning of the Torah

Mishnah: the written form of the Oral Torah

monotheism: belief in one God

Nevi'im: the words of the prophets in the Tanakh

Oral Torah: the set of oral laws handed down to Moses along with the Written Torah

pagan: one who believes in many gods

patriarch: a scriptural father of the Hebrew people

pharaoh: an Egyptian king

Pharisees: a Jewish sect that believed in the Oral as well as the Written Torah

Philistines: a people from Crete or Cyprus, known as the "Sea People"

Pirkei Avot: the section of the Mishnah dealing with the wisdom and ethics of sixty wise rabbis

pogrom: a deliberate attack on Jews and Jewish communities

Promised Land: the area promised by God to the Hebrews, located in southern Canaan

rabbi (RAB-eye): a sage or a teacher of the Torah

Renaissance: the period of European history from the fourteenth to seventeenth centuries marked by a flowering of the arts and literature and the beginnings of modern science

responsum: an answer given by rabbis to questions on Jewish law

Sadducees: a Jewish sect that believed in a literal interpretation of the Torah

Sanhedrin: an assembly of scholars acting as the supreme religious, judicial, and legislative council over Jews in Roman times; located first at Jerusalem, later at Yavneh

seder: the Passover meal

Semite: one who is said to be a descendant of Shem, the son of Noah

Sephardim: Jews who settled in Spain and Portugal

Septuagint: the Greek translation of the Hebrew Bible

synagogue: a Jewish house of worship and study that also serves as a community center

Talmud: the compilation of laws on ethical and legal behavior, as well as stories, parables, and sayings of sages; there are two versions, the Palestinian and the Babylonian Talmud

Tanakh (tah-NACH): the Hebrew Bible, comprising the Torah, Ketuvim, and Nevi'im

Torah: the first five books of the Bible: Genesis, Exodus, Leviticus, Numbers, Deuteronomy

yeshiva: a Jewish school for the study of the Torah and Talmud

Yiddish: an eastern European language based on German and Hebrew, colored by additions from many other European languages

Zealot: a member of a Jewish sect that rose up against Roman rule of Judea in the first century C.E.

Zionist: one who believes that Jews must have their own homeland in Palestine, or Zion

FOR FURTHER READING

Bachrach, Susan B. *Tell Them We Remember: The Story of the Holocaust.* Boston: Little Brown, 1994.

Chaikin, Miriam. *Ask Another Question: The Story and Meaning of Passover.* New York: Clarion Books, 1985.

Frankel, Ellen. *The Classic Tales: 4,000 Years of Jewish Lore.* Northvale: Jason Aronson, 1989.

Leder, Jane M. *A Russian Jewish Family.* Minneapolis: Lerner Publications, 1996.

Levitin, Sonia. *Escape from Egypt.* Boston: Little Brown, 1994.

Rossel, Seymour. *Introduction to Jewish History.* New York: Behrman House, 1981.

———. *Journey through Jewish History.* New York: Behrman House, 1983.

Schnur, Maxine Rose. *When I Left My Village.* New York: Dial Press, 1996.

Waldman, Neil. *The Golden City: Jerusalem's 3,000 Years.* New York: Atheneum Books, 1995.

Yolen, Jane. *O Jerusalem.* New York: Blue Sky Press (Scholastic), 1996.

The Holy Bible: New International Version. East Brunswick, New Jersey: New York International Bible Society, 1994.

BIBLIOGRAPHY

Barnavi, Eli. *A Historical Atlas of the Jewish People.* New York: Schocken Books, 1992.

Ben-Sasson, H. H. *A History of the Jewish People.* Cambridge: Harvard University Press, 1976.

Cantor, Norman F. *The Sacred Chain.* New York: HarperCollins Publishers, 1994.

Dimont, Max I. *Jews, God and History.* New York: New American Library, 1962.

Eban, Abba. *Heritage: Civilization and the Jews.* New York: Summit Books, 1984.

Fast, Howard. *The Jews: Story of a People.* New York: Dial Press, 1968.

Kark, Ruth. *The Land That Became Israel: Studies in Historical Geography.* New Haven: Yale University Press, 1989.

Potok, Chaim. *Wanderings: Chaim Potok's History of the Jews.* New York: Alfred A. Knopf, 1978.

Telushkin, Rabbi Joseph. *Jewish Literacy.* New York: William Morrow and Company, 1991.

Wigoder, Geoffrey. *Jewish Art and Civilization.* Secaucus, New Jersey: Chartwell Books, 1972.

INDEX

Page numbers for illustrations are in boldface

ABOUT THE AUTHOR

Kenny Mann has long had an interest in ancient civilizations and foreign cultures. She was born and raised in Kenya and lived for a number of years in Germany. She was a journalist and documentary filmmaker before turning her talents to teaching and writing books.

She is the author of *African Kingdoms of the Past,* a series of books for children about the history and cultures of Africa. She has also written *I Am Not Afraid—a Masai Folktale* and *Yellow Dog Dreaming*, a collection of short stories.

Today Kenny teaches creative nonfiction to young people ranging from fifth graders to college students. She lives in the quiet eastern Long Island town of Sag Harbor with her daughter, Sophie.